SARAH'S FIRST SOCCER GAME

by Alyssa Krekelberg
illustrated by Daniela Massironi

Tools for Parents & Teachers

Grasshopper Books enhance imagination and introduce the earliest readers to fiction with fun storylines and illustrations. The easy-to-read text supports early reading experiences with repetitive sentence patterns and sight words.

Before Reading

- Look at the cover illustration. What do readers see? What do they think the book will be about?
- Look at the picture glossary together. Sound out the words. Ask readers to identify the first letter of each vocabulary word.

Read the Book

- "Walk" through the book, reading to or along with the reader. Point to the illustrations as you read.

After Reading

- Review the picture glossary again. Ask readers to locate the words in the text.
- Ask the reader: How did Sarah feel before her first soccer game? How did she feel after? How do you know?

Grasshopper Books are published by Jump!
5357 Penn Avenue South
Minneapolis, MN 55419
www.jumplibrary.com

Library of Congress Cataloging-in-Publication Data

Names: Krekelberg, Alyssa, author.
Massironi, Daniela, illustrator.
Title: Sarah's first soccer game / by Alyssa Krekelberg; illustrated by Daniela Massironi.
Description: Minneapolis, MN: Jump!, Inc., 2025.
Series: First experiences
Audience: Ages 3–6.
Identifiers: LCCN 2023045598 (print)
LCCN 2023045599 (ebook)
ISBN 9798892130561 (hardcover)
ISBN 9798892130578 (paperback)
ISBN 9798892130585 (ebook)
Subjects: CYAC: Soccer—Fiction. | Teamwork (Sports)—Fiction. | LCGFT: Readers (Publications) | Picture books.
Classification: LCC PZ7.1.K7387 Sar 2025 (print)
LCC PZ7.1.K7387 (ebook)
DDC [E] —dc23
LC record available at https://lccn.loc.gov/2023045598
LC ebook record available at
https://lccn.loc.gov/2023045599

Editor: Jenna Gleisner
Direction and Layout: Molly Ballanger
Illustrator: Daniela Massironi

Printed in the United States of America at
Corporate Graphics in North Mankato, Minnesota.

Table of Contents

Part of the Team

It is my first soccer game.

My stomach twists.

I feel nervous.

"What if I mess up?" I ask.
"You play great at practice, Sarah. Let's go have fun!" says Kate.

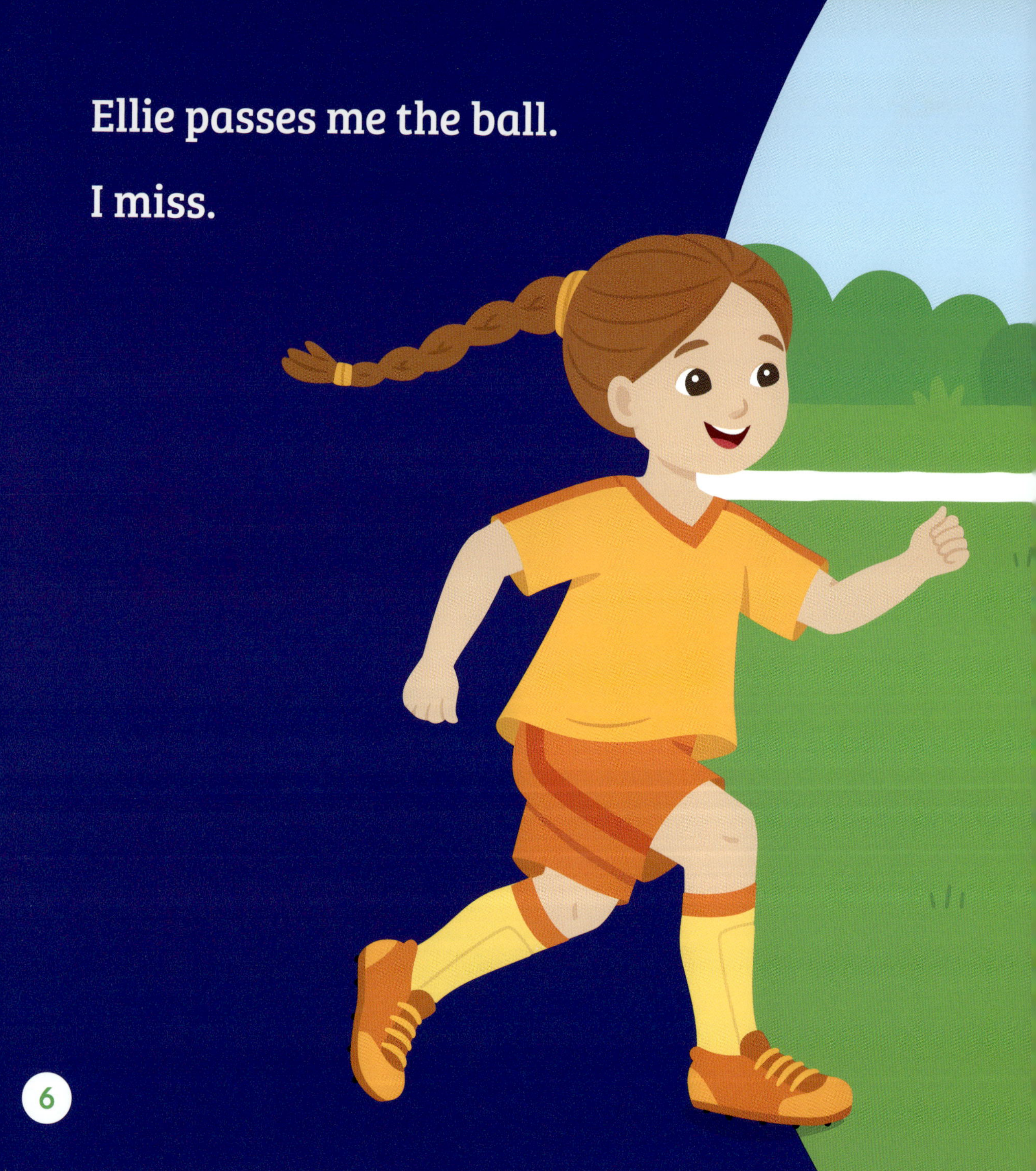

Ellie passes me the ball.

I miss.

The other team scores.

My heart sinks.

I wonder if my teammates are mad at me.

“I messed up,” I say.

“It’s OK!” says Ellie. “We are a team. We work together!”

I get the ball.

I take a deep breath.

I can do it!

I kick the ball.

I score a goal!

My teammates cheer.

We support each other no matter what!

Let's Review!

Sarah was nervous for her first soccer game. What did she do to feel better?

A. She talked about her feelings. **B.** She asked to sit out of the game. **C.** She yelled at her teammates. **D.** She did not give up.

Picture Glossary

nervous
Anxious or worried about something.

passes
Kicks the ball to another player.

practice
When members of a team meet outside of a game to work on their skills.

scores
Makes a point in a game.

support
To encourage or help someone.

team
A group of people who play a sport together.

Let's Review! Answer Key: **A.** She talked about her feelings. **D.** She did not give up.